Yes But What Is This? What Exactly?

Ian McMillan

smith|doorstop

the poetry business

Published 2020 by
Smith|Doorstop Books
The Poetry Business
Campo House,
54 Campo Lane,
Sheffield S1 2EG

ISBN 978-1-912196-37-1
Typeset by The Poetry Business
Printed by Biddles

Smith|Doorstop Books are a member of Inpress:
www.inpressbooks.co.uk

Distributed by NBN International, 1 Deltic Avenue,
Rooksley, Milton Keynes MK13 8LD

The Poetry Business gratefully acknowledges the support of
Arts Council England.

Contents

Introduction

Hello, and welcome to a collection of poems written in the depths of history, almost at a time before Time as we know it began. Yes, these poems were all written before the Coronavirus Crisis. I hope, though, that they speak to us about the concerns we had before the New Normal and will probably have when the New Normal becomes the Normal and then the Old Normal. Enjoy this glimpse into a contested and open-to-nuance past.

Tone Found in Sonnet: a Murder Mystery

Body found in suit.
Horse found in shore.
Hope found in hoopoe.
Man found in woman.

Foot found in sock.
Bats found in stab.
Wig found in wigwam.
Man found in Manchester.

Head found in hat.
Routers found in trousers.
Beast found in breast.
Man found in Godmanchester.

Ache found in heart.
Man found in Manitoba.

A Financial Crisis in Three Parts

1.

They smile before
They start the waterboarding
And so do we.

2.

I suddenly found
I lived in this house
But I didn't know
How I did it.
The instruction book:
I need the instruction book.

3.

He felt an almost overwhelming urge
To eat pound coins.

Between Junction 35a and Junction 36

The truck pulled up on the hard shoulder
And a curtain at the back opened theatrically
And they tumbled out, running
Into the evening-scribbled bushes like

Scattered chess pieces
Verbs cut from random magazines
Pepper ground onto cold soup
Marbles rolling across your grandma's yard
Billiard balls rushing somewhere over the baize.

Even the bushes were frightening
In a language nobody knew.

In the Bookshop: a Poem in that Ol' Plain Style

A man spends his book tokens
On a book that isn't one of mine.

The bookshop owner shows me
How the upstairs is a wilderness

That used to be a cake shop.
We've got plans. Reading groups,

Poetry sessions. There's a settee
Wreathed in dust, a chair reduced

To kit form. 'We need bookshops'
I say. 'I'm glad you're here.'

Downstairs the man is clutching
Military History to his heart.

He catches my eye and walks over
By the fiction.

Could I? Would you mind?
I wrote these when I was emotional

And printed them myself.
He passes me his book.

I ask him to sign it
But he already has.

Ten Der

The sound of flowers
Being snipped
In the other room.

She whistles,
Then she sighs.

She sighs,
Then she whistles.

The sound of tender
Murmurings
That could be song.

Adult Audio

My mother-in-law gathers two of my grandchildren
Around her tiny television
Like she is gathering peas that have been shelled.

'Yes, I've got CBBC,' she says. From a cabinet
Bearded me gazes down from my wedding snap;
That knife I'm holding is sharp. The cake.

My mother-in-law presses a button on the remote
Or should I say, I meant to say, she presses
The wrong button on the remote. Right remote,

Wrong button and audio comes on. The word
AUDIO loud across the screen. The grandchildren
Sit like chess pieces. 'ADULT!' my mother-in-law

Shouts, 'ADULT! I'VE SWITCHED ON ADULT!'
How slippery words are. How they cut
Like knives cut wedding cakes. The Shipping

Forecast calms its way out of the screen
On Radio 4. The ADULT shipping forecast,
Obviously. All those wet places.

The Fallen Christmas Tree at the Museum

Yes, you heard. It fell, even though
You and Aubrey had fastened it up,
Shackled it to the wall. The lights

Lit up the floor. The baubles were,
Let's see, how can I put this,
Bauble jigsaws, seasonal mosaics

And the angel just laid on the floor
At an angle to the world and looked
At the sky's starling-jam blankly.

Margaret came out and tried, successfully,
To sell me a raffle ticket. She said
'I won't write your name on the ticket

Because we all know who you are.'
Yes, Margaret, but does the angel?
Does the fallen angel know who I am?

Should I ask? Is the angel a whatsitsname?
A thingy? A metaphor. That's it. A metaphor?

The News

Headline or '... and finally'? You decide.
Go on, decide. You decide.

As I walk past the woman with
The white dog on a lead, somehow
I get tangled in the lead, one of
Those long ones that stretch
To Doncaster. I step over, or try,
And she lifts the lead and I trip
And then as I regain my balance I grab
A fence and she pulls the lead and
The dog tries to nip my trousers. I try
To step over again and she lifts the lead
High over my head but not high enough
And so I bend and crick my neck and
Try to step over the lead again and
Fail. We stand, still and still. The dog
Says 'Who's voting Tory on Thursday?
I know I am!' The lead is so long, so long.

Three Flat Caps at the Bottom of the Stairs

The mining industry, eh? What a bastard.
Men dropped at the speed of dropped kecks
Down a hole in the ground to land lamplit
And gasping. And now, what's left to ponder?

Just three flat caps at the bottom the stairs
Still there, years and years after he died.
Notice this: saying years and years piles them up,
Piles years on years like the coal the wagons

Used to pile outside the house. Take one
Of the flat caps and listen carefully: his breathing,
Like fingernails across wire mesh, like rain
On the bratish roof of a shed, still there

In that space behind the neb. Don't ever
Put it on. Don't let the grandkids put it on.
This is as important a cultural artefact
As that statue of Churchill or the Queen's head

You lick the back of every time
You send a card to a grieving widow.

Yes But What Is This? What Exactly?

1.

I snap my fingers at Time
Like it's a waiter
Approaching with soup.

2.

Rootling down the back of the drawer, I found these diaries from years that haven't happened yet. Rootling round the back of the diaries I found these drawings from evenings that haven't slipped by yet. Rootling around at the back of these years I found diaries that haven't been opened yet. Rootling around at the back of these evenings I found openings that haven't yet closed.

3.

This bit of the day was improvised
But this bit of the day wasn't improvised.
This bit of the day was completely improvised.
But this bit of the day was only partly improvised.
This bit of the day was improvised, but badly.
This bit of the day was improvised, but well.
This bit of the day was going to be improvised.
This bit of the day wasn't going to be improvised.

4.

Hello, Time. Tell you what:
You are like the fossil
Of a clown's last laugh.

5.

I think we'll start with a starter, yes,
We'll have (is distracted by the view
Of a bridge from the café window)
That, that thing, there, that thing
(Is distracted by the gulls flying over
The bridge he can see from the café
Window) that I believe (is distracted
By a memory of a rough trip to Lundy)
Is called, is called, soup. Please forgive
Me if I snap my fingers at you. I like jazz.

6.

I find that if I boil my egg for five years then I really can't dip my soldiers in. I don't know if this is a good thing or a bad thing because I have been alive for so long that I can't tell the difference any more.

7.

Time passes. It passes.
It passes. It scores.

8.

Dawn breaks with an audible click
And an owl waits in a bus shelter
For the first bus home. A man walks
A dog past me as I walk through the
Morning's paper hoop. Time, eh?
Time.

Lighter

'Sky's cameras appeared to show a fan of the home side making monkey chants at United's Brazilian midfielder Fred ...' – the Guardian, *9th December 2019*

You see, Sky catches everything. Everything.
That man stuck in a broken evolving door
With a tabloid headline for a soul. Later,

Spiralling through the noisy air, a lighter
Gathers darkness around itself, hits the floor
Which was not its intended target. Sing,

You only sing when you're not thinking
Of what gestures to make in the next moment
Of anger-fog as it swirls somewhere that leads

Here, to the movement of the limbs that bleeds
Out through the screen into my room. Ferment,
The cess-pit, the wound open and stinking.

Seeing a Goal Scored from a Passing Train

The train slows, almost stops. Drizzle's stories
Are stale and repetitious and the traveller
Wipes a hole in the window steam with his sleeve;

A goal is a brief moment of clarity;
A punctuation mark in a game's long sentence.

A match is happening on a soggily diluted field;
Men and boys run through sludge to get,
Well, where? To the future celebration, obvs.

A goal is a point of sudden change;
A new route found on an old map.

A bloke who looks like he is made of mud
Boots the ball so hard that the air,
The very air it travels through, almost breaks.

A goal is a memory you always knew you'd have
Even before the goal was scored.

The keeper flaps like a scarf in a breeze,
Wafts nothing except the ball's ghost
And the striker runs away, mouth open in joy.

The goal is always the goal of the game
And the goal of the season. Until the next goal.

I stand and whoop and the train's dullards
Stare at me like I'm a cave painting come to life.
I don't care. It's a goal. The train creaks, moves.

Lighthouses

That's what he said, in the interview:
'Let them live in lighthouses. After all
We have no use for lighthouses any more
So rather than having them litter the coast

Let the homeless live in them,
And then (chuckle in the voice)
When the light comes on it will seem
(giggle in the voice) like ... like ...

They have had a bright idea.'
Storms are the worst times.
The lighthouses shake and tremble;
Sometimes they blow away.

Too light, you see. Too (sob
In the voice) light.

Summer Dreams Ripped at the Seams

1.

A lad films his mate riding round a lawn
On a lawnmower; if this is cutting the grass,
Then, reader, I'm a flautist in a youth orchestra.
The circles he makes are like those a bird of prey
Etches across the sky. Anyway, the lad
Has already shared the film, may have already
Edited music onto it. It may have gone viral.

2.

A white van groans to a halt at 06.05
And a young man rushes to the back,
Creaks open the doors and two girls
In sunglasses and doll's clothing tumble out
And begin to dance to no music but the music
Of birdsong. The young man films the girls
And one of them grabs an empty bottle
From the gutter, bursts into spluttering song
Using the bottle as a microphone.
The young man shares the film, his phone
Reflected in those dark, dark lenses.

The Puddle

I'll tell you what writing a poem is like:
It's like this ...

Just the temptation to jump and splash
In the puddle at the end of the lane;
Like I was Ian McMillan aged seven,
In a knitted balaclava and shorts so long
They could have been a waterfall.

I stare into the puddle. A straw from
A McDonald's cup draws my eye. I grab it,
Raise it to my lips. I am tempted to suck
The entire puddle up and swallow it
But then I decide just to suck a portion

Of the puddle up, spit it out, and then
Suck it up again, and spit it out. The younger
Ian McMillan wouldn't have done this,
He'd have just splashed but as I've got older
I've realised the power of the redraft.

Where Was Your Ghost Before?

Taps chest. He was under this jacket,
This best jacket. Funerals, interviews.
That best jacket. He sizzled away
Like a tinnitus-riddle, waiting,
Waiting his moment. Taps head.

Sometimes he was here, brain area,
Humming because he didn't know
The words, just waiting, waiting.
That last shuddering breath: he'll know
And then, well, he'll blossom, shine.

Taps mouth. He sits in here, soaking.
He just waits for me to keel over
From underuse and rust. My mouth
Will open slackly. His song will emerge,
Keening, a high tenor. Tuneful? No.

Taps poem. He's in here. Always.